S0-AZU-727

This is a work of creative nonfiction. Some parts have been fictionalized in varying degrees, for various purposes.

Copyright © 2020 by Tyler Fuller

All rights reserved. No part of this book may be reproduced in any form on by an electrical or mechanical means, including information storage and retrieval systems, without permission in writing from the publisher, except by a reviewer who may quote brief passages in a review.

Book Design by Jessica Yanko
Illustrations by Jessica Yanko & Nate Brower

First edition of April 2020

ISBN: 978-0-578-67931-0 (paperback)

for the kid from the yellow house

Contents

Perhaps This Isn't a Suggestion

Introduction: The Day Before

this book is going to speed through at a strange pace
and I won't lie to you,
it's going to start off pretty fucking dark.

almost seven years ago when I first started writing,
I used it mostly as a coping mechanism.
I would write these sad little poems
about my dreams or longing for someone's touch.
I wish I could go back in time and punch myself
right in the fucking face
because I treated those situations like it was the end.
let me tell you, it gets so much worse.
so much fucking worse, and the moment
you realize that the easier it is to just start dying.

sometimes I sit on the floor in the shower
and let the water run cold,
hoping anyone finds me before I'm shriveled up
or before the water stops running altogether.
most days, I sleep long into the evening.
sometimes I don't even make it out of bed.
it's as simple and pathetic as that.
this time, I'm working in the kitchen
in the coffee shop in the center of town,
and Mike tells me I seem angry.
I don't believe I am, but maybe
he's goddamn right.

I mean, tell me Mike, have you ever
woke up to find pains in your legs
that you think couldn't possibly exist?
have you ever found scars against your skin
or fresh wounds, or dried blood,
and just ask yourself, "what the fuck?"
I'm finding my knuckles bruised and I'm tired again.
I feel like I should have some poetic, metaphorical brilliance
behind all of these things, I feel like after seven years
I should have more to say, but honestly,
all I'm feeling is exhausted.

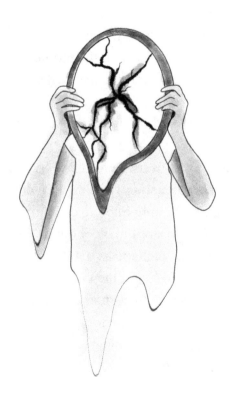

The Night Of

it's been
three whole years
since you hung the rope
around your neck
in your father's shed
and I miss you
every day.
tomorrow,
I will attend a funeral
for another comrade
who took his
own life
far too quickly.

what an incredibly
small, sad world.

Goodbye

when I stared at the
rock replacing a casket,
no words came.

when the funeral was over,
no one moved from their seat.

I realized that
we are all
directionless
now that
you're gone.

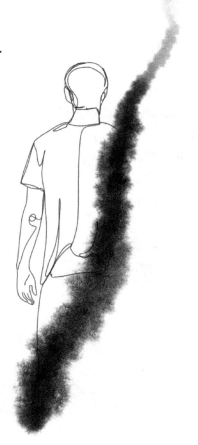

One Year Later

damn, how times have changed.
I haven't touched this journal in a year
back then I was getting drunk before funerals
& before that, it was months
between open mic at the local coffee shop
& before that, it was days
when I'd write late at night about love & loss
& before that, it was a day
or was it an hour
or was it a minute
or are we all just a moment,
passing.

Face Value

some nights I just want
to leave this all behind.
I want to toss everything
into the trash and disappear
into the alleyways.
I want to blend in
with the bricks
in the roads
and the creaks
in the doors.
I'm better off huddled
around trashcan fires
with people like me
who have no home
and no family to return to
than staring at my reflection
and wondering what monster I've become.

all of the people around me
have the same response to that.
"you wouldn't survive if you ran away."

Bruce Wayne did it,
and look how he turned out.

"that's the kind of shit
that's got us worried about you."

Constellations

I'm interested in thinking.
I think, you think, we think,
but we're not the same.
not at all.
and that scares me.

how we think is different.

I'm interested in thoughts.
I'm interested in the
unfathomable sequences
of random segments of ideas
mashed together to create
a singular thought.

Metacognition: thinking about thinking.
there are three doors;
behind door one there are three more doors.
same with door two.
and behind those doors,
there are three more doors
and so on until
you've created an entire map of steps
you could take with your thoughts.

what will happen once you make this move?
and after that move?

and that?
and that?
and that?
is that checkmate, and for whom?
because I'm drowning in left brain.

I can't breathe because
I'm thinking about how I'm supposed to.

and I can't tie a noose because
my hands won't stop shaking.

Dear God,

the bags under my eyes
are heavy enough
to bring me to my knees.
perhaps the church
can recommend
something for me.
the least I could do
is ask for help, right?
like with my problem of sleeping at night
or making it home in one piece
during car rides alone.
it's becoming difficult to keep myself
from wreckage,
my tendency to swerve
has increased because
I'm more concerned with
how I address myself publicly
than with how
I position my hands
on the steering wheel.

I've lost count of the times
I've made it home alive
and wished I hadn't.
it'd be easier
to just pull the wheel
and never have to worry

about fitting in again,
because compressed metal
and shattered glass
won't ask questions
I can't answer.

if there's a God, please hear me,
tell me you understand
because I'm having trouble
myself.

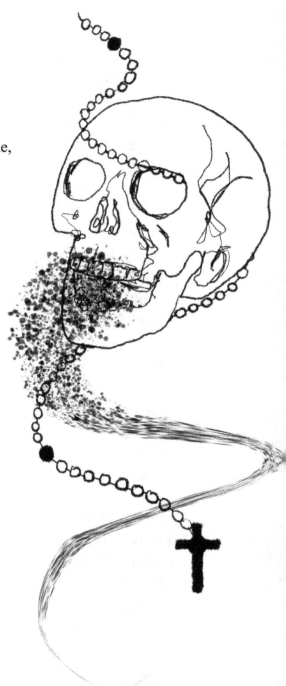

The List

when I was in a teenager
I struggled with my depression.
I made lists of ways to commit suicide,
different small, horrific ways to die,
and I'd like to introduce to you
the conclusion I found.

I could overdose (one),
self-induce comatose (two),
jumping off a bridge (three),
praying to whatever God you believe in
that you find your wings on the way down.
I'd want my body somewhere hidden
where nobody would find it until it was
rotten and untraceable.

have you ever called a suicide hotline?
when I was young I used to call
with blood running down my arm
and tears rushing down my face
and my father in the other room
thinking nothing's out of place.
and at this point, I hate rhymes.
I hate the way they portray my life
and what I feel inside and
I hate even myself.

I could slit my wrists (four),
take a train hit (five),
or even blow my brains out (six)
would you think to leave behind a suicide note?
leaving whatever to be your final words,
instead, I could tie my finger
to the trigger
and take a bullet to the skull.
but to be honest, that shit is messy
and I'd hate for someone to have to clean up
my scattered thoughts.

I've noticed we judge others for judging others,
so hate me because I hate me.
I've spent many months
just agreeing with what others say,
but is this process effective for me
to find peace?

I bet nobody told you that
when you overdose
your muscles could start to spasm and leave you paralyzed
or if you tie a noose just a little off perfect (seven)
it might just snap your spine.
even the easy way out isn't easy.

I could drink bleach (eight)
or not respond to that chain e-mail (nine)
okay, I'm joking on that last one, but what if?

my list is still going strong and I am almost out of fingers
faster than it would take an ambulance to get to my house
if I popped a bottle of rat poison (ten)
or if I downed a bottle of tranquilizers (eleven)
and watched life drag itself out of my skin
and left my body behind, and suddenly
the whale that washed up on the beach
when you were nine doesn't seem so funny anymore.

still making this list, and the truth is
I don't know if I'll ever crash my car into a pole (twelve)
or fill my coat with stones and attempt to backflip into a river
(thirteen).
because, honestly, there is so much to love.
I could get lost for hours at a pond, just watching the water
move.
I could take the time to learn to fish, to swim, to dive,
to live a healthier life.
I can get lost for hours sitting on the roof of my garage.
I can get lost at a coffee shop, at a bookstore,
at the record joint, climbing the silos at the edge of town.
I could just get lost, man. it's the little things every time.
it's easy to get taken away with life
so for each way I've found to kill myself,
I believe I'm finding another to live.

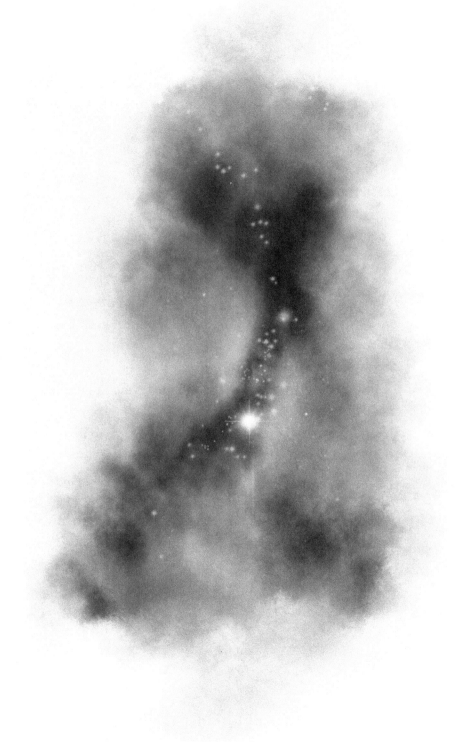

Recycle

we sipped our drinks
played basketball
and later that fall day
I took my cousin Zoe
longboarding around town.
we took the backstreets
away from traffic
to the park
and finally
to the cemetery.
we rode downhill
on what felt like
fresh pavement
past a few hundred gravestones
and under the two trees
right to where his headstone stood.
we stayed for a while
as I blabbered
and pondered
what could have been
if he hadn't called it quits.
at some point
Zoe asked me
"would you rather be buried
or turned to ashes?"
I said that
when I die,

I want to be
turned into
a tree.
and that kinda sounded
like fairy-tale, so
I started doing research.
there's this thing called a
"Bios Urn,"
a biodegradable urn
made from coconut shell,
compacted peat and cellulose
containing
the seed of a tree.
once your remains
have been placed
into the urn,
it can be planted
and then
the seed germinates
and begins to grow.
there is a comfort
in knowing that
my death
will not just be
one more nail in the coffin
of the earth.
worst case scenario:
after my family has gone
and my leaves have fallen

and our names
carved into my bark
have worn,
I'm cut down
and turned into paper,
into books.
back into stories.

Focus

there are things I need to spend more time focusing on.
the road instead of my phone.
the placement of my hands on the wheel.
where I put my keys (pocket? attached to my hip?)
how sunrises and sunsets make me feel.
the joy of watching someone talk about their passions.
the first snowfall of the season.
the wonders of shooting stars.
splashing in puddles on a rainy day.
the feeling of being held in someone's arms.
how Christmas lights can be utilized any season.
the way dogs get excited when you return home.
how often wearing shoes isn't necessary.
how easy it is to put a smile on someone's face.
the beauty of clumsy first kisses.
the warmth and loveliness of fresh laundry.
the way music makes me feel.
the sound of good laughter.
how often I tell my friends I love them.
how tightly I hug someone goodbye.
how little time I have.
how little time we have.

Seasonal Depression

I'm terrified of what winter
will bring this year.
I haven't had it checked but
last winter was really bad.
I think it could be
seasonal affective disorder.

it's chilly in the back of the shop today
and I'm debating making a fire
out of signature receipts,
making us all s'more lattes
and holding on to the smell of campfires
and the crunch of autumn leaves.

I'm at a loss for energy so
I close my eyes for a second and
hear waves crash against the sand.
I'm standing in Lake Michigan,
the water's freezing but
everything seems so endless.
I run my palms across the top of the water
and feel some connection to
the distance between waves
until I hear Xavier from the beach
yelling, "you crazy bastard, you'll freeze!"
which wakes me from my daydream.
now it's just cold, no connectivity,

the shop is empty,
and I feel worse than when I started.
I hope this is just because of winter.

please let me blame it on
the weather.

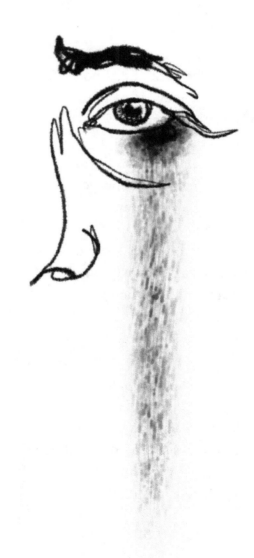

Picture

in my desk drawer,
I have a leather journal
with a photograph of you
on the cover,
pinned down
under the elastic strap.
I don't really write in it much.
when inspiration strikes,
I usually take it out,
stare back at you,
then feel tired.

I'm going
to bed now.

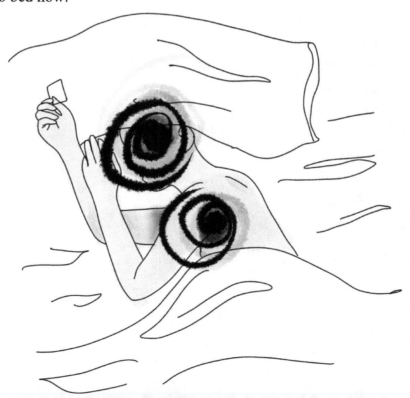

Supervene

I saw your car
follow me down
my street
one night
as I was coming home.
when I noticed,
it pulled over,
made a three-point turn,
and drove the other way.

the other night,
your car was
tailgating me
on the expressway.
I'm pretty sure
I saw you parked
at the grocery store
and out on the street
the other day too.

it's true
that you start
noticing things
after they're
gone.

You

all the stars in space
outnumber every
word
spoken by
every human
that has ever lived.
but every star
and every word
that any human
has ever said
wouldn't measure
to the time
I'd waste
trying to write a poem
for you.

Good Morning

I fell asleep
on my arm again
and thought you were there
sleeping beside me
cutting off
my circulation.
I woke up
still numb
and
still smiling.

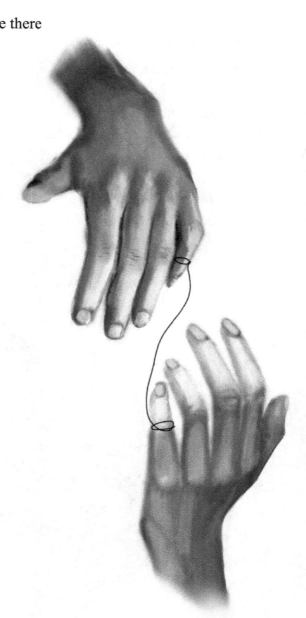

Matter

I wish you were here
so I could tell you
about all the stars
within your eyes.
there are a billion universes
in the grooves of your hands,
the gates of heaven
can be found resting
on the soft of your lips.

come here and show me
how nothing ever mattered.

Lovely Words

I have always wished to be a painter.
I was cursed with the ability
to only write poems and short stories
about sadness and love.
I just want to be able to paint a scene.
like right now,
I sit a foot away from you on the couch,
your messy blonde hair flowing down
your shoulders. your delicate, tanned legs
exposed below your shorts.
you paint at the dining room counter,
your brushstrokes swaying back and forth
like the weeping willow tree that I would read under
on Howe street. you've painted a lilac sky
cut deeply with blue streaks,
bushes of pink sprouting from the foreground.

I am by no means a painter,
but you are the sight I can share with the world
in words.

City Streets

I stopped writing poetry
because of the places it took me.
lately, I've been getting back into it
she's been taking my hand
and walking me through it
the city streets that live
in between the grooves of my hands
worn down and ravaged
by sickness and death
have installed streetlights
since she laced her fingers between mine.
funds were donated to house on 131st
with the rickety wooden steps
and boarded front window
so they could remodel
they added new gutters and a green trim
and the neighbors are happy about it.
the truck stop off 231
added a soda vending machine
all the kids go there for
when they decide to play football by the church
or when they drink out by Skip's Pond.
there are two middle schools now.
it's great because it gives the kids a sense
of rivalry, but also
more families have been moving to town.

I started writing poetry again
because the industry has been saved.
she's been taking my hand
and walking me through it
and each time she does
this town feels a little more
like home.

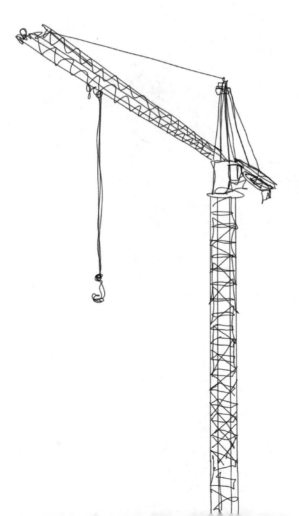

Stars

before I met you
I had trouble
sleeping.
even in our
early days
I'd spend hours
after you dozed
staring at
the ceiling fan.
I'd lean close
and trace
with my finger
the freckles
on your stomach
a soft map
of the Little Dipper
and wonder:
do I thank
the stars
for you?
or do I thank
you, for you are
the stars?

Notes

I'm going to start leaving myself notes around the house.
something little, something I'll quickly forget
but which will help me get through the day when I read it.
I'll start by writing something like "looking good!"
on the cap of a water bottle before class,
or a "today is a new day" to throw into my bag.
hell, maybe even draw a smiley face on the toilet seat.

sometimes all we need is a little push to keep going.
it's hard to say out loud but allow yourself to remember
that it's all going to be okay in the end.
don't be afraid to speak your thoughts.
we all live with insecurities,
but some of us have fears that others don't
so find those who have courage and they will teach you.
they will teach you that you don't need to be afraid,
that you can be anything you want to be.
for years, I've wanted to be worth listening to
and I just started believing I am
because the note on the mirror told me so.

and maybe it's that simple for some of us
and if so, just be happy because
things could be worse.

Oh, Happy Day

Mood Indigo by Louis Armstrong
in the back of the shop.
90° on the first day of fall.
my girl is on her way
with tobacco so I can
roll more cigarettes.

oh, happy days
soothe you
like smooth jazz.

Youth

it's a reoccurring theme
in horror films
where children would
pull their covers over their heads
when they went to bed
to protect them
from the monsters of the night.
when I was young
I would fall asleep
with my hand over my heart
thinking I could catch it
if it ever tried to
fly out of my chest in fear
and then I would be
brave enough to face the night.

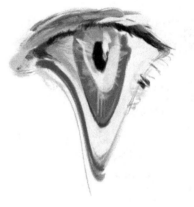

but the older I became
the only thing that changed
was the harder
I clenched.

New Suit

my girl took me out
to buy a new suit
the whole nine yards
pants, shoes, coat
my first new suit
in almost a decade
and I felt good.
when we got home
she had me try it on
and she took pictures
and I felt damn good.
she left for a meeting
so I undressed, took off
my coat and dress shirt.
then I heard the crash.
two cars collided
outside of my apartment
metal and glass scattered
across the block.
I ran out the door
in my dress pants
and suspenders.
I pulled a woman
from of the driver's seat
while her head
bled into my hands
and I stayed with her until

till the paramedics arrived.
apparently the daughter
was down the street
and I slipped away
when she turned up
and watched her mother
loaded onto a stretcher.
later I rolled a cigarette
and tried to remember
how good it felt
to buy a new suit.

Omen

there is a strange accord
between wolves and crows.
the crows help the pack find their next kill.
the wolves leave a portion of the kill
for the crows.
the crows chase and are chased
by the wolf cubs for their pleasure.

which begs the question:
when you spot a crow,
is it a bad omen?
are the superstitions true,
is bad luck upon you?
or are you one
of the wolves?

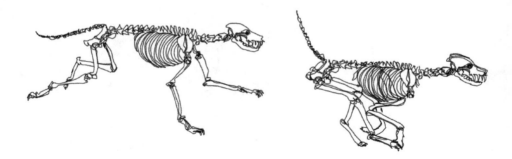

Purpose

I worked as a bouncer at a nightclub
in my early twenties.
it was a powerful,
menacing
environment.

on busy nights I was guaranteed
at least one fight to break up.
on dull nights we'd tend to have
few patrons or none at all
to keep an eye over.

when there were few
we would post at certain spots,
near the bar or in the corners, hidden,
watching,
waiting for someone to slip up,
waiting to bury our fangs in flesh.

when there were none
I would read and sometimes write
until eventually
I noticed the bartenders
snickering at me.

it was a powerfully
menacing environment.

Yet To Be

time is becoming
slow and dull.
nights spent drinking
whiskey from plastic cups
in this college bar
leave me tired
as do nights spent indoors
with literature
and jazz.

I am either
yet to be satisfied
or this life altogether
has become
slow and
dull.

Incapable

the bar patio is infested
with bees.
it must be the sugar spilled
by the mixed drinks,
I suppose.
they fly, curious and irritated
around the patrons, my college peers,
delta omega fraternity assholes,
and women dressed to show their smooth skin
hoping one of these terrible excuses for men
will try and take them home
after more spilled drinks.
they all are loud, crazed and drunk
but the bees do not sting.
they never do.
the bees and I are one and the same.

Deduction

do you ever wonder if
some people are born for greatness
and others are born to live
sad, pathetic lives
and work dead-end jobs
or live day-to-day with no purpose
just to make those great people
seem greater?
if everyone has a destiny,
what if mine is to write
sad, pathetic poems
so that you will remember who is
truly inspiring?

Last Night

last night you told me
we were going separate ways
and I wandered the snowy streets
wishing I was dead.
I went to the bar
I used to work at
and downed too much rum.
then I walked and smoked
and cursed the night.

I walked the streets
asking strangers for forgiveness
until I was back at the bar
and Nolan told me
maybe it's just not my month.
when I got home, still drunk,
I was planning to hang myself
with my old leather belt
but you were there
asleep in my bed
so I put blankets over you
and smoked at my desk
realizing our last night
would have been my last night
if you hadn't stayed.

tomorrow you'll be gone
maybe for good
but I'll wake up
and thank you
for waiting.

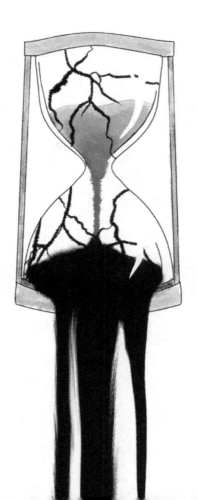

E-Cigarette

I received an electric cigarette
from a colleague
she said that it is
better for my teeth
better for my gums
better for my lungs
that it has
a higher nicotine content
today my girl left me
I'm working late at the bar
my bones ache
I have writer's block
and I want
a real goddamn cigarette
I want to feel
a warmth in my chest
where I feel cold.

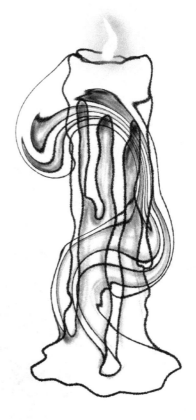

Far, Far Away

I lay upon layers of stardust
and I hear the voices of our children.
I see the light through tattered curtains,
the truth doesn't always concern what's right.
the answers all stand before me,
seeing through to you and you to me and we
never knew what "I love you" really meant.
you're close to the bottom of your bottle,
I'm a few thousand light-years away
drifting on unfeeling, dark limitlessness.
what we always needed
was space.

Lonely Words

I have always wished to be a painter.
I once loved a woman
who didn't have many motivations
other than painting
and drinking liquor.
she always saw the world
from an abstract perspective
from the wood of her brushstrokes
from acrylics & happiness
from the bottle always
half full with cheap rum.
she stopped loving me
because I didn't understand
the importance of Picasso or Van Gogh
the importance and usage of color mediums
the expressionism she created
after painting beautiful
delicate lilac skies.

I pour whiskey into the mug
she dipped her brushes in
grab a cigarette
sit at my desk in my leather chair
take a long pull of
liquor & paint chips
and describe to you this setting
in lonely, colorless words.

Simple

you don't always find meaning.
there are no answers
at the bottom of my flask.
she wears black, lacy underwear
because she wants to.
he has no televisions in his home,
and he reads. because he enjoys to.
I called you because I wanted to hear your voice,
and you didn't answer, because
you must not have wanted to.
I brought my fifth of bourbon
into the shower with me
and sat on the floor until
I drank myself to sleep.
these are just simple, sad things
that happen all the time.

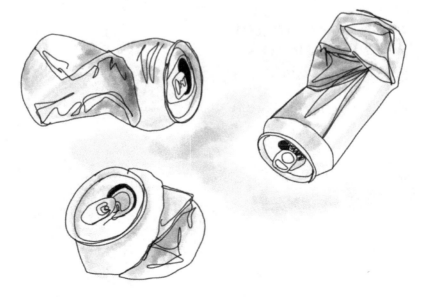

Illuminate

Luna used to invite me out at night
where I'd meet the crickets.
I met some great musicians.
we used to sit in the fields
and listen to these insects
practice for shows.
I'd sneak a flask in my coat
when Luna brought me to the concerts.
I'd always offer to share,
but she was never really into the scene.
the harmonies they produced
really knocked her out of orbit,
but that was the only thing
that distracted poor Luna
from the thrill of the chase of the Sun.
I told her, "alcohol is a great way to forget someone!"
she was upset by my suggestion.

perhaps this isn't a suggestion
and also not anything else,
so I stopped offering.

Traffic

she used to kiss me at red lights.
I would make her coffee in the mornings
and maybe leave a note under the mug.
some mornings, I wouldn't even have time
to make myself a coffee
because I was running late to class.
we would sleep in too often.
she would crawl out of bed,
with her blonde hair shining in the light
from my window, her soft smile poking through
the top of her shirt as she tossed it on,
and would run with me out the door to her car
to make sure I got to class on time.
now, I get to class early,
I have a coffee every morning,
and red lights last
twice as long.

Building

I love
much like
how I build a fire.
I throw in everything
I have ever owned
& accidentally
smother it
before it ever had
the chance
to breathe
and let us
feel the
warmth.

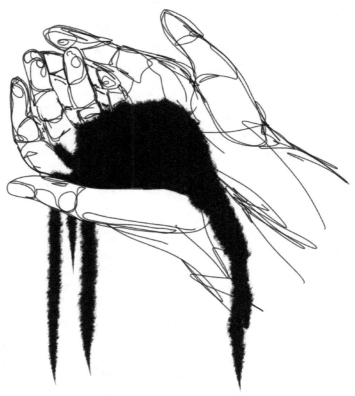

Submerge

fire, water
& love
can all
suffocate you
once you're
lost
within them.

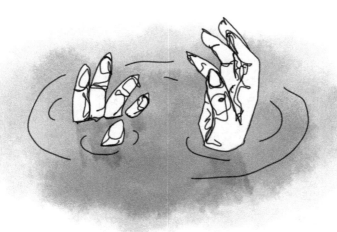

Closure

she lost the key, she told me,
it must've fallen out of her purse
when she dropped the rest
of my things into my unlocked car.
it was my own fault, really,
waiting so many months before
asking for my life back,
but still, fifteen dollars to replace,
I told her.

what, are you serious, she said,
won't management replace it
for free?
fifteen dollars, I told her.
fuck you, she said,
you asshole!

I hung up the phone
finished my beer
and watched the end
of the Patriots game
at the bar down the road
but when I got home
there were fifteen dollars under the mat
so I went inside
fed my cat
lit a cigarette

and then walked down Walnut
to the liquor store
to buy more booze
with the fifteen dollars.

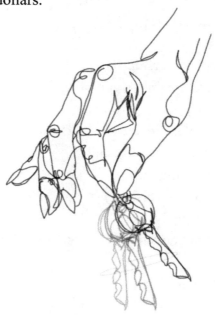

Insanity

one of my colleagues in high school
was known for preaching endlessly
about the importance of
freedom and
love without ownership.
I thought him a helpless end of an era,
a wild rabbit
within the violent food chain
that the rest of us would climb.
I stopped smoking grass
and moved on to whiskey.
I left for college
and I heard he moved to Oklahoma.

during my senior year
I ran into his sister.
I was working the nightclub
and she arrived with the DJ.
from when the night was young
until last drinks
were called
she danced alone,
and I finally understood.

they were
mad and free
and I was

alone
with my whiskey.

Life

several times
there are moments involving movement
and other times
the stillness is the happening.
in this instance,
everything is happening
at once.

Love Letter

I write to you, the woman at the bar,
with your smooth, tanned legs leading to your tight jean skirt,
a grey crop top showing your petite breasts through thin fabric,
lips glossed with red under blue eyes,
your straight brown hair swept to one side
and some stubbly man standing close on the other:
are you finding happiness at the bottom of those cheap liquor
shots?
are you finding happiness from the spouting from this man
who can't hold himself stable without the support
from our brown and black wooden bar stool?
are you happy knowing your own allure
draws men from drunks to poets to take part in noticing you?

do you think that I could find any happiness
in knowing you will never read this?

Promotion

on slow nights while
working as a bouncer
at the local bar
I would read and
sometimes write
and the bartenders
and the runners
and the goddamn customers
would exchange looks
and converse without words:
"that crazed son of a bitch!"
"why can't we enjoy our drinks
in peace?"
"get him outta here!"
and they did.
one day I was promoted
to kitchen staff
with a significant pay raise.
I understood
what really happened.

they thought they could
hide me in the kitchen
where my thoughts
would not hurt
anyone again.

Assistance

the birds sing in C minor.
the birds sing in C minor
on the power lines
outside of my apartment
while I smoke cigarettes
in the stairwell.
the crows scare them away
around noon,
because they know
I can't think straight
with those fucking birds
singing their songs on mornings
I didn't want to wake to.

I crack an egg into my beer
sit at my desk
and thank the crows
for their help
in clearing my head.

Brick in the Road

on my walk home
from the bar
I trip over a surfaced brick
and I ponder if
it is coincidence
or bad luck
whether it's the city's fault
or my own
for being this drunk
on a Monday night.

I take a right on Grant
instead of Lincoln
to avoid the homeless
who camp outside
the public library
after hours
not because I hate them
but because
I don't want to
fuck with them tonight
they've had enough
shit going on
and I haven't any
cigarettes to offer
to make sleeping
huddled together

with torn strangers
in a parking lot
any more bearable.

I trip a second time
outside my apartment
and decide
it's all probably
bad luck.

Similarity

moths are always looking for the moon.
they navigate by maintaining a
constant angular relation to its light.
but when a moth encounters an artificial star,
like this lamp beside my bed,
it instinctively attempts to correct the angle
by turning toward the source,
usually resulting in a spiral flight path
getting closer and closer to the bulb.

so everything in this moth is telling it
to smash its body into hot glass.
it's doing the right thing, but
it's just the wrong light.

funny
the similarities we share
with insects.

The Beast

my bones are brittle
they pop and they crack
every morning
when I wake
to the beast
beside my bed.
can we take a break today,
I beg.
you didn't let me sleep
last night and I'm drained.
please leave me be,
I don't want
to see the light again.
but the beast
bites into my ankles
and drags me
through the hallway
and the kitchen
through the living room
out the door
and into the day.

that son-of-a-bitch!
the beast has burdened me
with another day.

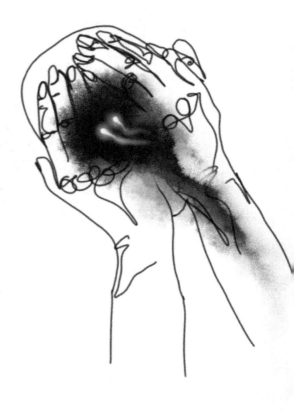

Rinse

I've heard that somewhere
in the mountains
in a hidden corner
of the world
there are hot springs said to
cleanse you
of your darkness.

I'd like to
travel there
someday.

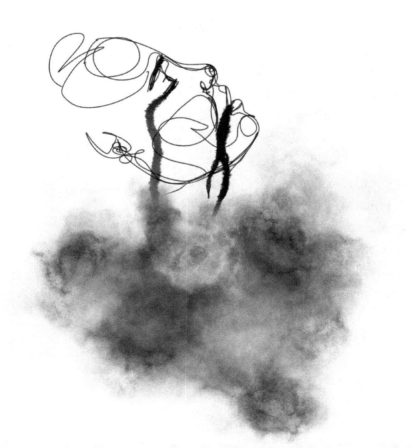

Twenty-One

I drove three hours North
to be at the cemetery today.
it's been six years
since my friend hanged himself
and it was forecast to be
cold and wet
but it was
sunny and bearable
when I pulled up
near the headstone.
I grabbed my lawn chair
from the trunk
along with a beer and my smokes
took a seat
and offered him a drink
he would have been twenty-one
so I poured a third of my Coors
into the soil and fall leaves.

it wasn't long after
I'd made myself comfortable
that his dad drove up
in a green truck
with orange words on the side
I assume he came straight from work
he brought flowers
we talked for a bit

and I offered him a drink
but he declined.

then I asked a stupid question
I said, do you come here
on his birthday?
he stared at me so I rephrased it,
do you come here
on his birthdays
or his death-days
or both?
times are hard now
and I was genuinely curious.
he looked at me and said,
I'm his father.
he put his hand on the headstone
and the tears cultivated over years
of pain and loss
fell while I observed
in silent mourning.
he gathered himself to leave
and said to me,
you know, he would have been twenty-one.

after he left I got my answer.
he comes here
every day.

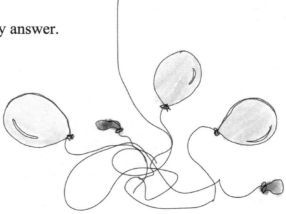

Bagels

up is a lot like down
when the only options
left are right, he says.
what the hell does that
even mean, I ask
the poor bastard,
this mad hatter
sitting next to me
at the bar counter
and he laughs.
here's another one, he goes:
a bagel and the earth
are a lot alike, however
a bagel is missing
its core.
I tell him to piss off
and let me finish my whiskey,
and he tells me
I am the bagel.

I still ponder that one
from time to time.

Black Holes in Your Bedsheets

it's very dark.
my foot is
out of the comforter
overhanging the bed
but it doesn't feel anything
from the overhead fan.
you sleep tenderly,
breathing deeply
with your head
nuzzling my neck
while I sit and trace
the bumps on your back
with my fingertips,
trying to make
constellations.

across the room
I see movement
in the shadows.
it's probably nothing.

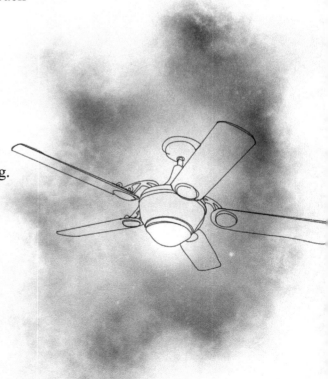

Night at the Bluebird

I forgot to roll
any cigarettes this morning.
I was too hungover.
I had a date last night
at the Bluebird
and she stayed the night.
we didn't fuck
but I slept wonderfully
she woke us up
thirty minutes before my alarm
so I went down on her.
she let herself out
while I got ready for work.
I was running late
and I ran out the door
without any cigarettes.

Into the Wild

going mad from isolation
and
falling madly in love
are the first steps
into the wild.

Teaching

today, at work, I burned
two trays of breadsticks.
the head cook called me out
on the first order but
let the second sit and burn.
he knew damn well they were burning
and he damn well could have saved them
but he decided it was better
to teach me a lesson.
he slaps me on the wrists and smirks,
"I hope you learned something valuable today."
afterwards, he left to have a smoke
and I had to roll another goddamn
tray of breadsticks.

Thankful

heading home for a few days
around Thanksgiving
it was bitter and snowy
& I was angry about it.
my sister had to drive
three hours
to get me from my apartment
because my piece-of-shit car
wouldn't start
it's got to be an electrical problem,
it has to be,
I just installed a new battery
and the brake lights still work.
anyhow, by the time we arrived
at our mother's house
everyone was asleep
the dogs kept barking
and I was afraid they'd wake the others
so I grabbed some books
& walked through snow
to the pub for a beer.

some drunks eyeballed me,
probably for carrying
literature & I saw some guys
who'd fucked with me in high school.
I didn't say hello.

I sat at the counter
& talked to Gina the bartender.
she's always been my favorite.
she's been serving me since seventeen,
I ask her, three-fifty for a Miller, right?
three-fifty was all I had.
times were rough.
two-twenty-five, she said.
I tipped her the rest anyway
while some brunette questioned me
about my books
and her boyfriend laughed at me
from across the bar.
that dumb son of a bitch.

later Gina got on the intercom
& yelled at those fools who
fucked with me in high school
to stop sitting on the pool table
or she'd overcharge them
& I laughed.

I was young & poor
& times were rough but
it was good to be
home.

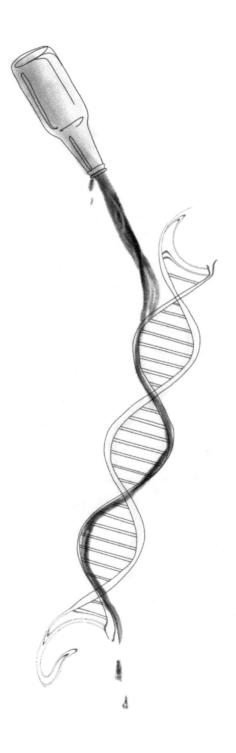

Traditions

one night after returning from the windy city
I went to surprise my father at his favorite bar.
when I got there the place was pretty dead
and I was clearly out of my depth.
someone asked me if I was looking for trouble.
I said I was looking for whiskey.

I took a seat and asked about my father.
apparently he'd already gone,
but I could feel the small crowd warming towards me
and they began to share their booze and stories.
so I hung out with my father's friends,
Bob and Rob and Maddy and the rest.
Rob told me a story about a drunk man
who wandered into the bar looking for a fight
so he broke a beer bottle over his head
and dipped before the police arrived
to be honest, I liked Rob a whole lot
short stack of a man, but he really showed.
I wondered whether what they say is true,
that you turn into the people you turn towards.

Sky Lantern

I was rolling cigarettes inside the house
when my mother insisted
I join the others outside.
it was dusk and the frigid air chilled the town.
my uncle had started a fire in the yard
and everyone was filled with laughter and booze.
my sister brought out a sky lantern
and the crowd went fucking wild.
it's easy to please midwesterners.

my uncle's girlfriend, Thea,
gathered everyone together
and called forth all of our
negative emotions, our stresses
and placed them inside of the sky lantern.
she proclaimed it was time for us all
to let go and move on
peacefully.

my mother lit the flame that would
carry the lantern into the night.
my sister took it into the yard and
let it go. it soared
briefly through the air,
freighted with our feelings,
straight into the tree beside the garage.
strangely, no one moved.

there was no sense of urgency.

I lit my cigarette and laughed
as I watched the worry I'd been
fostering those past few years
burn my garage to ashes
and I kept on laughing hysterically
like a crazy person
until the fire department arrived.

Healthy

I used to have
shit to write about
while working at the bar,
when I rolled my own cigarettes
and the sun beat down while
working the outside patio of the bar.
I used to break up fights on the daily.
I'd come home to dried blood on my shirt
feeling damned good.
now it's cold,
I'm bothered by the idea of conversation
because I have nothing of substance to say
so I wallow in an anxiety of sorts
and I try to keep to myself for the most part.
I've been moved to the back of the kitchen
and I've shriveled up,
hiding during my smoke breaks
inside the crevices between bricks
for our walkways nearby the bar entrance.

I've learned every damned recipe
in this damned establishment
so I distract myself with
how to cook a good quesadilla
or a batch of salted fries
to stop myself from
putting my head in the oven

or bludgeoning myself with a knife
or jumping off the roof onto the spikes
around my beloved bar patio.

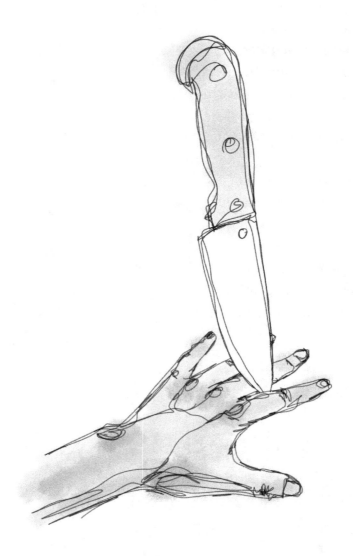

Don't Stop Spinning

this year for Christmas
I received rent money
and a titanium top.
I have yet to understand
the latter's significance.
even now, I spin and spin
this tiny, metal toy
waiting for the poetic brilliance
to speak to me
whisper, only to me
through its curves
and still-moving illusion.

I don't really get it
but I'm writing again
so I believe it's filled
its purpose.

Resolutions

I'm going to try
to write more this year.
my brother gifted me
a notebook and a new pen
in hopes to free me
from my moods.
I've started smoking herb again.
the clutch went out on my car.
my cable got suspended.
I've fallen further behind
on my rent.
today at the bar
Nolan asked if I'd made
a new year's resolution
and I told him
I'm just going to try
to write more this year.

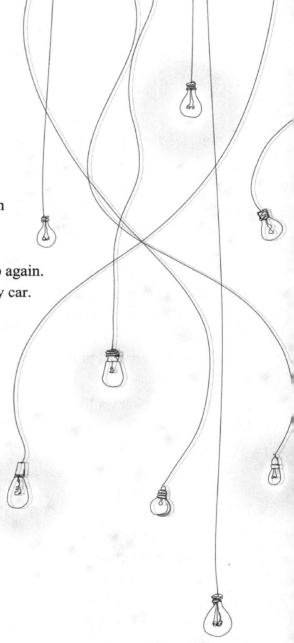

Walk Again

you took me home from the pub
back to your place
your roommates
were at some college party
so it was only us
drunk and free
to take a hot shower
at two in the morning
taking turns rubbing soap
on each other and
it was the very first time
I saw you naked
so I took you to the bedroom
and went down on you
until you begged me to fuck you.
we went through
the last two condoms
and I held you
until the birds sang to us
in the early morning
when you woke up
you told me you'd dreamt
that we were married
but I was paralyzed
from the waist down
I laughed and joked about
this being a strange fantasy

and you told me
you would be there
every step of the way.

Recipes

it wasn't long after being
promoted to the kitchen
before the managers
started watching me.
before I became lazy
& unkempt. I stopped eating.
I had no hunger.
I just yearned for
a feeling.
but management swept me
from my searching
& sat me down
to dissect me with
tiresome questions.
they listed my positive
& negative qualities:
he's always in a good mood.
he's knowledgeable.
he's reliable.
he takes long breaks.
he's been caught drinking on the job.
he has been caught writing on the job.
finally they asked,
"do you hate this job?"
so I told them
a moron is limited
to the assembly line

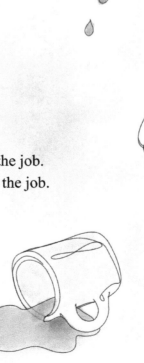

but a genius can master astrophysics
or deliver mail.
a genius can become
a cardiologist
or a bus driver.
I don't hate my job,
but with my promotion
came my frustration
& I wonder
well, which am I?
am I the moron
or do I have potential?
at least when I was a bouncer
I could take out my aggression
on drunks who overstayed
their welcome.
I abruptly left the meeting
& they promoted me to server.

the bastards got me.

Learning

there's not a book
in any library
on this earth
that will teach you
who you are
& what you're
meant to be.

Dreamer

summer moon.
bright as winter day.
Luna watches over
the sinners,
the lovers,
the fighters,
the poets,
the greedy,
the poor,
the few,
the many.
I realize now
that it is not enough
to hear; the moon
will only talk to those
that listen.
she howled to me
when the wolves
were silent:
"in order to love yourself
you must first know
who you are.
to understand
is to transform
what is."

Searching

all of humanity
is searching for
truth
justice
& beauty.

we keep on searching
because we fail
to see
that everything
is already
within us.

Nocturnal

if you ever feel lost,
take pride in the accuracy of your feelings.
ask your doctor, "why?"
"why do my words seem frail
yet my thoughts so powerful?"
do not stop asking your doctor this.
repeatedly ask, "why?"
as you slump, sedated, into uniformed arms.
leave the office
smiling
because not all who wander
are found.
but do not forget
the questions
left unanswered.
and don't forget to set your clocks forward.
don't forget to confuse time with numbers.
don't forget the vastness of space.
don't forget what you don't know yet.
look at me.
let me be clear.
let me be entirely unseeable.

sometimes the point is lost
with the presentation.

Medication

if you're happy and you know it,
the chemicals are finally working.
are you seeing double?
are you starting to notice the creaks in
your floorboards when no one is walking them?
if so, ask your doctor about... them.
also, that shadow?
dancing from side to side when you try to sleep?
possible side effect.
possible cosmic entity stripped from the void,
doomed to drift in the unwelcoming nothingness.
I'm sure everything will be fine.
please go back to thinking of other things while
they monitor your vitals.
just kidding!
but please breathe slower,
for the machines.

Memento

when I got the letter
that I was accepted into the university,
I stayed up all night and waited
for my father to return from the bars.
at three in the morning, he stumbled in,
and when I showed him the letter
he had tears in his eyes
we stayed up for another hour or so celebrating.

when I finally left for college,
he gave me this straw hat
that he used to wear when he was my age.
he said,
"you're gonna be a great man someday."

three years later I dropped out
and returned home, the embarrassment
of the family but I still wear
that straw hat.

Nicotine Was My Obstetrician

I've lived my life in an ashtray.
the color of the smoke has changed
over the years, but
not the smell. not the sight of
cigarette-stained smiles.

my mother has always been good about it.
she always smoked outside.
when I was a kid,
my father used to flick his cigarettes
into a small black jack-o-lantern ashtray
stemming out of the ground
by the back door.
I used to climb the support beams
and accidentally kick them out,
spilling cigarette butts all over
the flowers.

when my grandfather passed
my father started smoking
in the room with the television
sitting in the same olive and white
cotton armchair his own father
sat in before him
what seemed like every day.
the jack-o-lantern ashtray
now lays on its side,

uprooted from the ground,
buried under dirt and grass.

I sit beside my father,
inhaling nicotine like life hasn't
changed us, watching the Bears lose
Sunday after Sunday,
like nothing has changed at all.

Barkeep

sometimes I miss
more than anything
working as a bouncer.
the environment
kept me sharp
& gave me a place
to vent my rage
on assholes
who got too physical
after too many drinks.
now I'm soft,
I haven't fought
in months
& I'm angrier
than ever.

Few Words

solitude
is one of
the few words
that can both
comfort
& terrify.

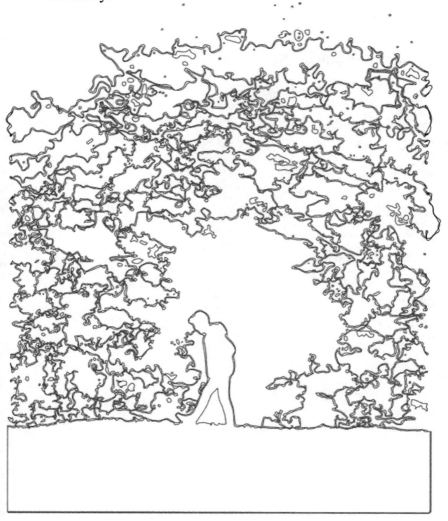

Queen

on a bus to Chicago
I met a guy who said he was
the current boyfriend
of a woman married
to one of the members
of the band Queen.
I took it with
a grain of salt
but he shared with me
three smokes
while we waited
at a stop outside
Indianapolis
and in forty-five minutes
of waiting
we discussed
politics, poetry,
academics, passions,
love, loss, pain,
our dreams
& our worries.
others came &
begged for a smoke,
to offer drugs
or to fuck us
in exchange
for a bus ticket.

I told them each of them
to fuck right off,
but he shared
his cigarettes anyway.

later we returned to the bus
& sat several
rows apart.

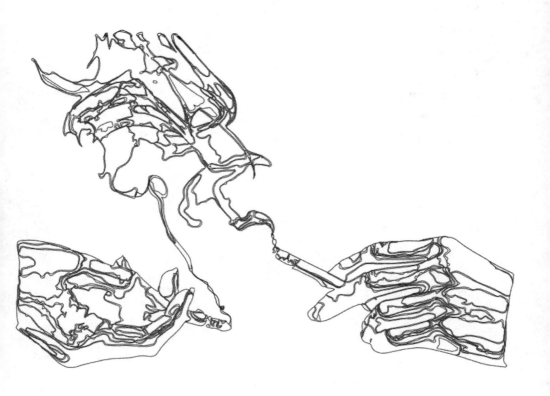

Cheers

in the bleak mid-winter
I was working a double
serving drinks
in a near-empty bar
one of our regulars came in
ordered a shot and a beer
and sat alone
for at least an hour
so I drank with him
he started crying
he said his buddy
from the marines
took his own life
leaving behind his wife
and two children
and he couldn't fathom
how he could do that
to them or him
he kept muttering about
how many friends
he's lost like this
he ordered two shots of whiskey
and asked me to
leave one of the shots
on the counter
for the rest of the night
he slammed his hands

on the counter
and cursed the moon for rising
he cursed his friend for dying
he cursed football players
for getting paid millions
when the people who serve
end up at the end
of a fucking rope
finally he
grabbed the shot on the counter
and asked if I would say something
for us to raise our toast.
I poured myself a shot of Irish
raised my glass to meet
all of his finite memories
but it doesn't matter
what I said.

Standing Still

I finally quit smoking cigarettes
now I chew on toothpicks
whenever I have a craving
so tonight I stand in the snow
in slippers, sweatpants & my big coat
chamomile tea still lingering in my throat
with a mint toothpick hanging out my mouth
staring up into the sky
at a very beautiful lunar eclipse
barely visible through the clouds
but all I can think about
is how much I miss sleeping beside you.
the winds burn against my bare face
so I finish admiring the night & step inside
hang my coat in the closet
collect myself at my desk
pour myself another cup of tea
& write you a message
that I'll probably never send.
it's a very lonely feeling.

Same Old

in high school
I had a small side gig
delivering pizzas
around town.

in college,
before working
as a bouncer,
I delivered sandwiches
to the campus drunks.

after I dropped out
I moved from bar to bar
until a buddy got me a job
in a warehouse
for an electrical contractor,
delivering pipes and parts
to electricians
around the county.

life is funny
in a sad way
that
things
never really
change.

I'm always
going somewhere,
giving people
what they want,
always returning
to nothing.

Animals

we're all just
animals
at each other's throats
going absolutely mad
in love
with the thrill
of the fight.

Going

often while driving
I am not paying no attention
to the road;
my hands grip the wheel
and I just go.
I do not read enough anymore.
I do not drink whiskey.
I do not write.

and so I continue
to drive,
void of any feeling,
longing to get
anywhere.

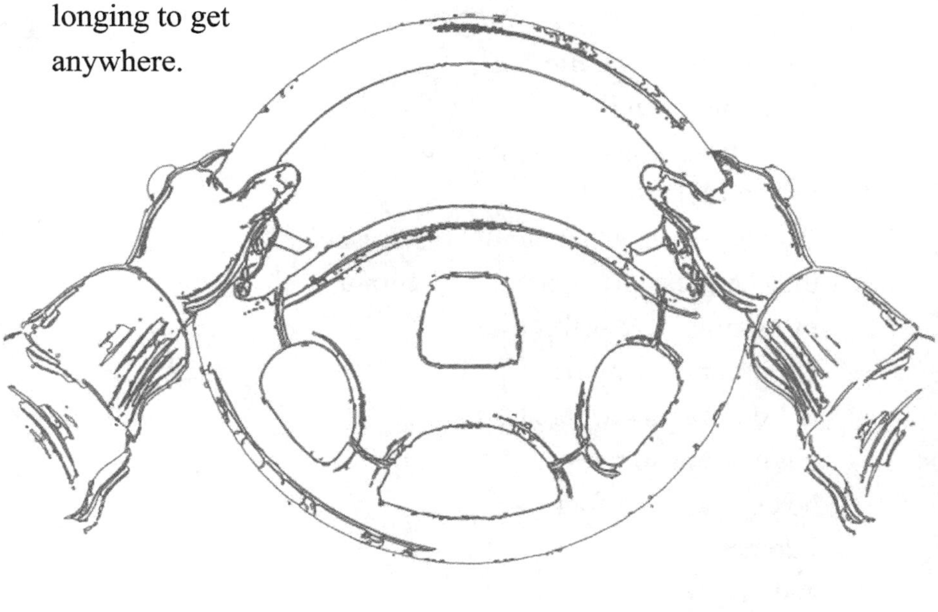

I Wonder

Hotel La Salle on Hohman Ave
laughs at me from above
as I head towards the bridge
overlooking the train tracks
in my rusted Ford pick-up
& all the small city buildings
are stained with dust & dirt
that even this rain can't wash away
the skies are dark & morbid
my windshield wipers are on full blast
I'm waiting for the train to pass
& watching a man under an umbrella
stand on the sidewalk by the tracks
he smokes a cigarette
with long inhales
as the train whirls past him
he's entirely too close
& he just stands there until he's finished
then he flicks his cigarette at the train,
turns around, & walks away.
I don't know why he waited
& I don't know where he's going
but it seems to me
he knows something
I do not
and maybe
never will.

Godspeed,
my friend.

Visor

this morning on my drive from work
there was an elderly man collapsed
in the right lane off Columbia
cars were accumulating, people were
crowding around him
the car in front pulled over
and a woman rushed out
to help, phone in hand.
a bystander in a motorcycle helmet
with the visor down
stepped up to direct traffic
and as it became my turn to pass,
I did.
does that make me a bad person?
I mean there were enough people there
a crowd was forming for Christ's sake
I would have just been in the way
and I don't think I could have really
done anything for him.

I watched the scene get smaller
from my rear-view mirror
and by the time I had gotten home,
I had forgotten all about it.

Historians

nothing good has come
of these past few years.
no political justice for the poor.
no role models.
no poetry.
I wonder what historians
will think of us.
will they portion us
into decades
like the '80s and '90s?
or will they get lazy retelling us?
will they lump us together
in hundreds, or thousands,
picking out only the salvageable
from this worthless era?
I won't be included in these stories.
neither will you.
and they still won't have poetry.

Little by Little

my older brother once told me
I was just a product
of my environment.
that I was too hard on myself
for falling into
this abyss of devoured youths.
that it happened to tons of people
our age.
but he grew up, went to college,
moved to LA,
joined the video game industry,
worked on an interactive web-show,
won an Emmy, met the love of his life,
started his own company, got married,
goes to conventions all over the country,
and lives happily with three cats
and a corgi in West Hollywood.
he told me to do anything I could
to run away as fast as possible.
to be quicker than quicksand.
"go back to college, get your degree,
be what you want to be,
write that book you've always wanted to write,
make a name for yourself,
and if you can't, do manual labor,
sweat, bleed, and cry into your bank account,
join a union, become a journeyman,

flip burgers, buss tables,
sell flowers outside a cemetery—
do whatever you have to do and
get out alive."

that day the only thing going through my mind
was how little money I would make
selling those damn flowers.

Survival

living life, writing poetry,
waking up and doing the damn thing
every single day,
filling pages and pages
of this journal,
has taught me one thing:
Bukowski had it right from the start.
the world doesn't spin right
unless you're fucking or fighting
like a lunatic. whiskey & good music
can help.
but what's the point in living
when you're not.

Acknowledgments

First and foremost I would like to thank every single one of you for taking the time to read my first collection of poems. I have been accumulating them since I started writing during my sophomore year of high school. I just feel the need to voice how appreciative I am to you for reaching the end of the book, for reading these lines, and I hope some of my poetry resonated within you. I've had my share of trauma concerning the death of loved ones, falling in and out of love, alcoholism, and depression, but writing has been a constant in my life and it is so exciting to finally share with another person all of these things. I am forever grateful.

I would like to thank my high school poetry club, Windfall, for setting me off down this path. When I walked into my first meeting I had no idea how far I would take these lessons later in life. The first time I read my poems aloud I shook so hard I dropped my papers, but soon I was hosting open mic nights at the local coffee shop and giving kids a place to speak freely. And now I've written this book. That was all thanks to you. Keep poetry alive.

To my family: I could not have done any of this without your love and support. We have not always seen eye-to-eye, and there have been too many counts of disconnections over the years, but I was only able to come this far thanks to your tough love and guidance. Although I haven't finished college yet, I hope being able to say your son is a writer makes your heart as warm as it makes mine. Mother, Father, Justin, Julie, Amber, Ally, I love you all very dearly.

I would also like to thank the incredible Olenik and Rebey families for welcoming me into their hearts in my time of struggle during my adolescence. Family is not limited to blood relations— you have all shown me that time and time again. I am eternally grateful to every one of you. Mr & Mrs Olenik, Mr & Mrs Rebey, Haley, Zoe, Matthew, Sarah, Melissa, Logan, Adam, Grant, Charlotte, I wish to be a part of your family forever.

I am greatly appreciative of my close friends who have helped me in times of high anxiety and stress. Who knew writing a book would be so difficult! Steven Potosky, Shelby Sell, Zack Donaldson, Taylor Jagiella, Stephanie Sotiropoulos, Eric Heritier, Dom Emerson, and Willie Bennett, thank you for your companionship. I am incredibly lucky to have you as a part of my life.

The following people read drafts of this book and offered in return their critical insight: Joseph Dosen, Alyssa Amaloo, Abbey Nielson, Grant Arnold, Steve Savich, Sydni Weisbrodt, Jessica Leake, Lexi Summers, Jade Reeves, Sophie Meagher, Grace Landry, Justin Reynard, Julie Wilson, and Sarah Rebey. They gave me their ears and their hearts and they helped to make this book better. I thank you all for your excellent advisory council and your compassion. I could not have done this without you.

My editor, Luke Allen, was a tremendous help in getting this book through production and during our time working together he had passed along some knowledgable goods that I will continue to adhere by. My work with him was short but incredibly enlightening and I am in his debt. Grateful wouldn't even begin to explain how I feel for having worked with him. Thank you truly.

Finally, thank you to my illustrators, the wonderful and talented Jessica Yanko and Nathaniel Brower, who have both spent much time tediously dealing with the shambles that is my mind to create artwork for these pages. It had not been easy, but it was a pleasure discussing what this book would eventually become with you two. I am so happy with the outcome and I know you are as well. I hope you continue to follow your passions wherever they lead.

About the Author

Tyler Fuller is a young American writer, poet, amateur painter, jazz enthusiast, motorcycle rider, full-time cat dad, a fan of morning yoga, and a contestant for the title of "world's largest Adam's apple." He grew up in Northwest Indiana and studied English at Indiana University for some time before returning home to be with family. He lives in Highland, Indiana with his cat Barbara. This is his first book.

CPSIA information can be obtained
at www.ICGtesting.com
Printed in the USA
LVHW081252160520
655725LV00026B/1953